The DINOSAUR Files

THE AGE OF
GIANTS

text *by* Olivia Brookes

WINDMILL
BOOKS ™

New York

Published in 2012 by Windmill Books, an imprint of Rosen Publishing
29 East 21st Street, New York, NY 10010

Illustrated by Gary Hincks, Steve Kirk, Nicki Palin, Peter Scott,
John Sibbick, and Studio Inklink,
Illustration copyright © John Sibbick 13C

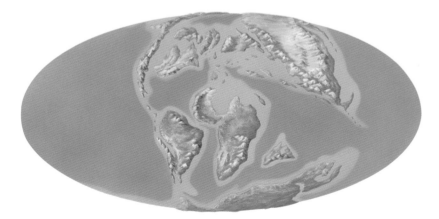

Library of Congress Cataloging-in-Publication Data

Brookes, Olivia.
The age of giants / by Olivia Brookes.
p. cm. — (The dinosaur files)
Includes index.
ISBN 978-1-61533-518-3 (library binding) — ISBN 978-1-61533-524-4 (pbk.)
— ISBN 978-1-61533-525-1 (6-pack)
1. Dinosaurs—Juvenile literature. I. Title.
QE861.5.B755 2012
567.9—dc23

2011022836

Printed and bound in Malaysia

Websites
For Web resources related to the subject of this book,
go to: www.windmillbooks.com/weblinks
and select this book's title.

CPSIA Compliance Information: Batch #OW2102WM: For further information contact Windmill Books, New York, New York at
1-866-478-0556.

Contents

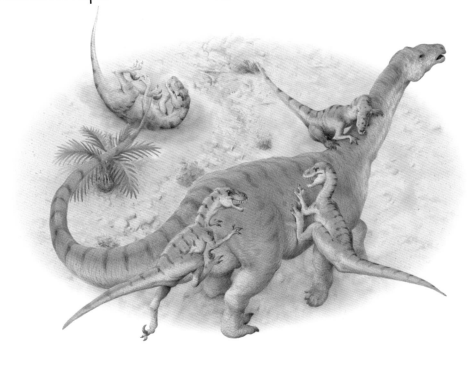

DINOSAURS ruled the world for 165 million years. Modern humans have only existed for about 100,000 years! These animals were some of the largest and fiercest creatures ever to walk the Earth. It is no surprise that the name "dinosaur" means "terrible lizards." No other large land animals existed from about 230 million years ago until the dinosaurs disappeared 65 million years ago.

During the Age of Dinosaurs, hundreds of dinosaur species evolved or died out. Some were gentle giants, others were vicious predators. Many were tiny, no bigger than cats. A few could run as fast as an ostrich today.

Most reptiles, including today's lizards and tortoises, walk on crooked legs positioned at the sides of their bodies, but dinosaurs walked on straight legs. Dinosaur species are grouped by the shape of their hip bone. The first group is the Saurischian ("lizard-hipped") dinosaurs. Saurischians include all the theropods (meat-eaters), and the giant, plant-eating sauropods. All other dinosaurs, many with armored plates or horns, belong to the second group, the Ornithischian ("bird-hipped") dinosaurs.

Drifting Continents

THE OUTER SHELL of the Earth is made up of large slabs called tectonic plates, which make up the continents and the ocean floors. These plates move slowly at

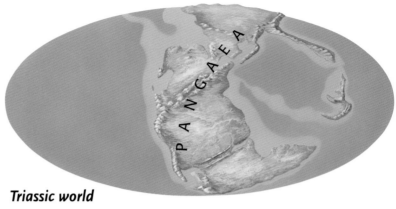

Triassic world

a rate of about half an inch (1 cm) per year. About 200 million years ago, the continents came together to form a supercontinent called Pangaea. The Americas were connected to Africa and Europe. Since then, the continents have split apart again.

Ocean floor

Heat flows

Mantle

CORE

CRUST

Continent

HOW DO THEY MOVE?

Heat flows through the mantle, a part-solid, part-liquid rock layer below the Earth's crust. The heated rock rises towards the crust, then moves sideways, causing the tectonic plates to spread apart. When the rock cools, it sinks again, reheats, and the cycle continues.

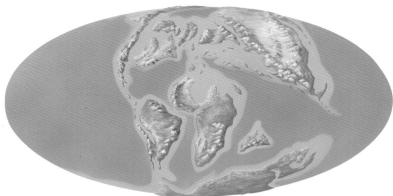

Jurassic world

CHANGING WORLD
These maps show what
the world looked like and
how it changed during
the 165-million-year Age
of the Dinosaurs. In the
Triassic period, all of the
main continents were
joined together in the
supercontinent of
Pangaea. During the
Jurassic period, the
continents began to
move apart. Pangaea
separated into Laurasia
and Gondwana. Sea
levels rose, flooded the
land, and then fell again.
So the shapes of the
continents changed too.

Cretaceous world

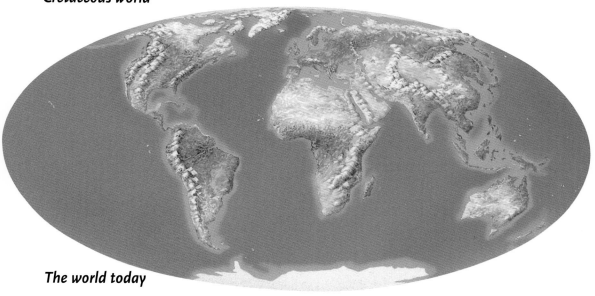

The world today

The Story of Dinosaurs

THE STORY OF THE DINOSAURS began about 360 million years ago when some kinds of fish learned to crawl on to land. These animals, the first amphibians, kept close to water, where they laid their jelly-covered eggs. It took another 50 million years for some creatures to find a way of laying their eggs on land. The reptiles had evolved. By the Triassic period, 230 million years ago, some reptiles ran around on two legs: these were the first dinosaurs *(below)*. The plant-eaters evolved from these flesh-eaters. They started off on two legs, but, by the Jurassic, had grown so big they had to walk on all fours.

Most of the story of the dinosaurs takes place during two geological periods: the Jurassic and Cretaceous. The Jurassic (opposite, above) was the heyday of the gigantic sauropods, like Diplodocus. The birds evolved from a group of small, feathered theropods in the Jurassic period. The Cretaceous (opposite, below), saw the rise of new kinds of plant-eaters, some with armor or spikes.

1 Coelophysis
2 Plateosaurus
3 Lystrosaurus
4 Ornithosuchus
5 Proterosuchus

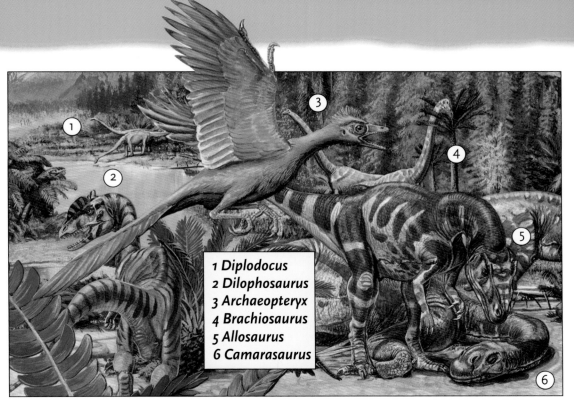

1 Diplodocus
2 Dilophosaurus
3 Archaeopteryx
4 Brachiosaurus
5 Allosaurus
6 Camarasaurus

1 Iguanodon
2 Styracosaurus
3 Corythosaurus
4 Tyrannosaurus
5 Struthiomimus
6 Morganucodon

THE AGE OF DINOSAURS began with the Triassic period, 251-200 million years ago. All the land on Earth was joined together in the supercontinent Pangaea surrounded by a great ocean called Panthalassa. So the world looked very different to how it appears in maps today. Some lands were in completely different places: India lay between Africa and Antarctica, far from the south of Asia, where it lies today.

TRIASSIC SOUTH AMERICA

During the Triassic period, the world's climate was warm and dry. Only the toughest plants could grow. One of the first dinosaurs was Herrerasaurus, a fast, 6-foot (2 m) hunter living in South America almost 230 million years ago. Riojasaurus was a 1-ton (1 t) plant-eater that lived here 10 million years later. Meanwhile, in Europe, the long-necked plant-eater Plateosaurus lived peacefully—that is, until Ornithosuchus attacked. Tiny Saltopus was no threat. Just 2 feet (61 cm) long, it fed on worms and bugs.

PANTHALASSA

NORTH AMERICA

SOUTH AMERICA

PANGAEA

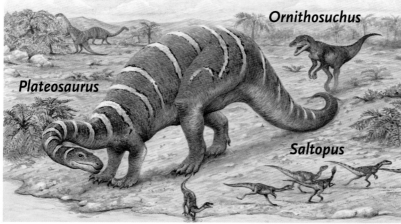

Ornithosuchus

Plateosaurus

Saltopus

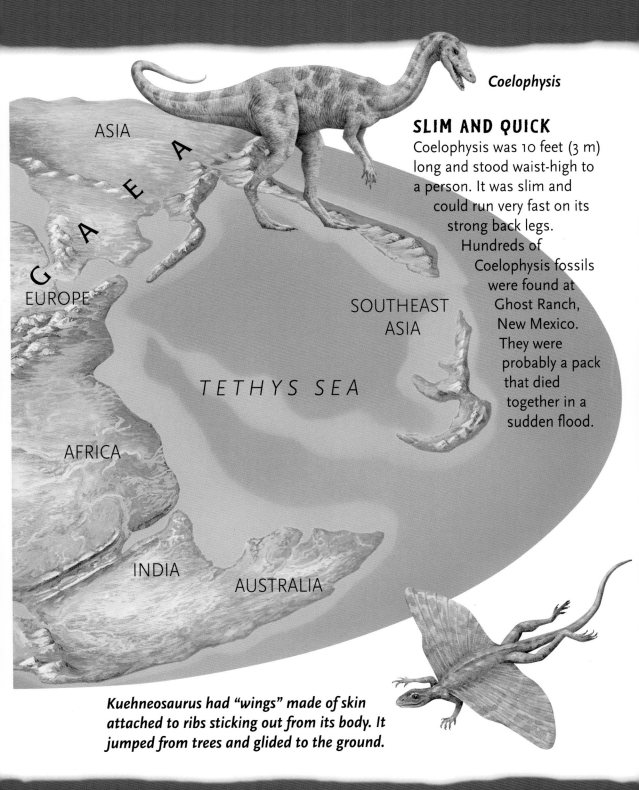

Coelophysis

ASIA

G A E A

EUROPE

SOUTHEAST
ASIA

T E T H Y S   S E A

AFRICA

INDIA

AUSTRALIA

SLIM AND QUICK

Coelophysis was 10 feet (3 m) long and stood waist-high to a person. It was slim and could run very fast on its strong back legs. Hundreds of Coelophysis fossils were found at Ghost Ranch, New Mexico. They were probably a pack that died together in a sudden flood.

Kuehneosaurus had "wings" made of skin attached to ribs sticking out from its body. It jumped from trees and glided to the ground.

Jurassic World

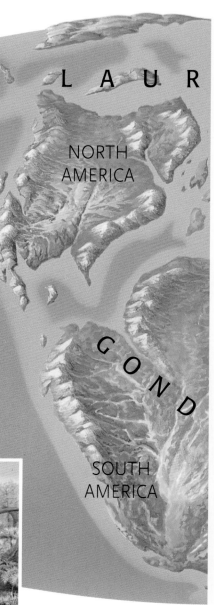

DURING JURASSIC TIMES, Pangaea started to break apart. Laurasia in the north became many smaller islands. In the south, Gondwana formed one big continent. The climates changed, too, as these landmasses gradually moved. Many places grew wetter, and plants, such as conifers, were plentiful. Large, plant-eating dinosaurs thrived on so much food.

JURASSIC AFRICA

Some of the biggest Jurassic dinosaurs lived in Africa. One was Giraffatitan, a brachiosaurid with long front legs and a long neck. It was 80 feet (24 m) long, 40 feet (12 m) tall, and heavier than 10 elephants. Kentrosaurus, a stegosaur, was a smaller African dinosaur. About as big as a car, it could "stick up" for itself. The strong bony plates on its back served as armor while the sharp spikes on its tail were a deadly weapon. Like Giraffatitan, it was a plant-eater, but it could only reach plants growing close to the ground.

L A U R

NORTH
AMERICA

G O N D

SOUTH
AMERICA

Giraffatitan

Kentrosaurus

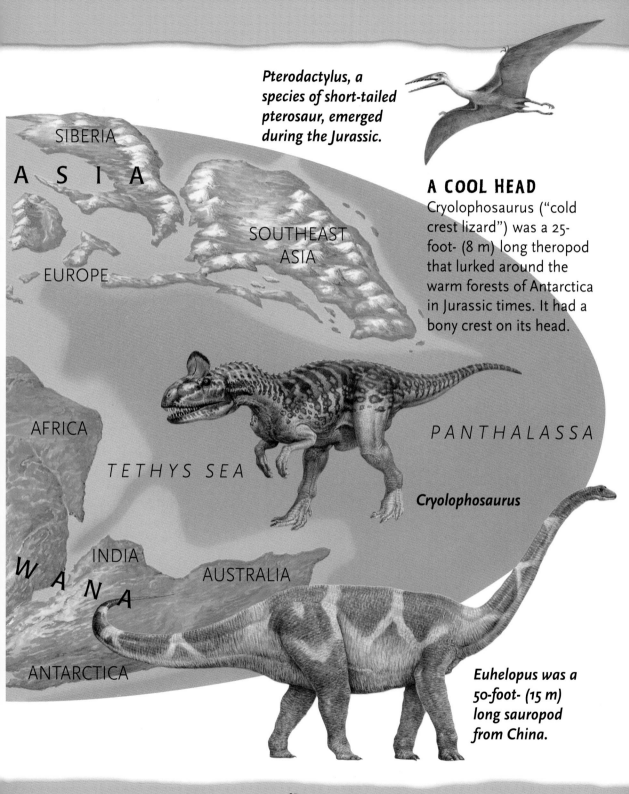

Pterodactylus, a species of short-tailed pterosaur, emerged during the Jurassic.

SIBERIA

ASIA

SOUTHEAST ASIA

EUROPE

A COOL HEAD

Cryolophosaurus ("cold crest lizard") was a 25-foot- (8 m) long theropod that lurked around the warm forests of Antarctica in Jurassic times. It had a bony crest on its head.

AFRICA

PANTHALASSA

TETHYS SEA

Cryolophosaurus

INDIA

AUSTRALIA

WANA

ANTARCTICA

Euhelopus was a 50-foot- (15 m) long sauropod from China.

Aleutian
Islands

GREENLAND

EUROPE

PANTHALASSA

NORTH

AMERICA

MEXICO

AFRICA

SOUTH
AMERICA

D URING JURASSIC TIMES, the Atlantic Ocean separating North America from Europe had not yet fully opened up. There was also no link between North and South America, as there is today. The polar regions—what is now Alaska and Canada—had no ice or snow, even in winter. In the forests that covered vast areas of North America, conifer trees, such as redwoods, grew alongside ginkgo trees.

LIFE IN THE MUD

Many parts of Jurassic North America were covered in muddy swamps and marshes. Here, the giant sauropod Diplodocus, along with the shorter but heavier Apatosaurus, stripped leaves from tall trees. Stegosaurus had tall plates of bones on its humped back. These plates could have soaked up the sun's heat, making it warmer and more active. It swung its spiked tail to defend its young against fierce predators, such as Ceratosaurus.

Ornitholestes

Raptors were a new group of meat-eaters in Jurassic North America. They had a huge curved claw on each foot.

Utahraptor

Ornitholestes was a small meat-eater that fed on lizards, frogs, and insects. It also ate larger hunters' leftovers.

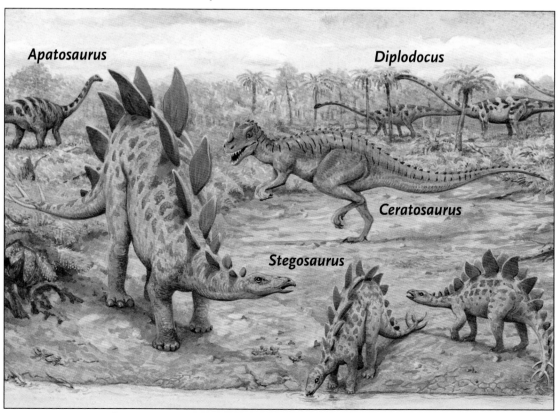

Apatosaurus

Diplodocus

Ceratosaurus

Stegosaurus

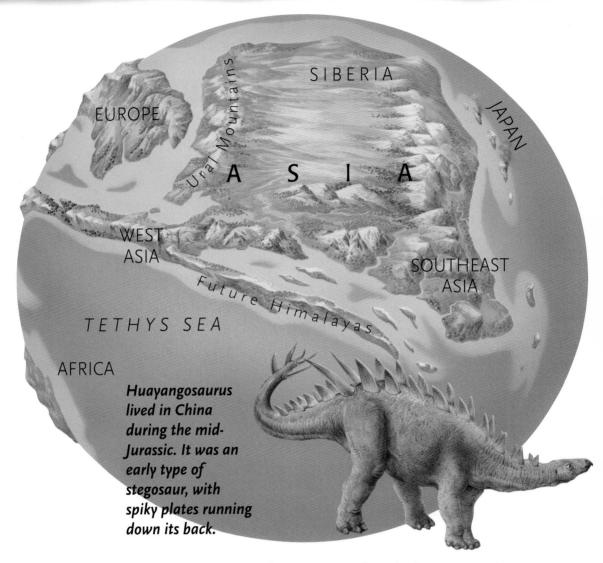

SIBERIA

EUROPE

Ural Mountains

JAPAN

A S I A

WEST
ASIA

SOUTHEAST
ASIA

Future Himalayas

TETHYS SEA

AFRICA

Huayangosaurus lived in China during the mid-Jurassic. It was an early type of stegosaur, with spiky plates running down its back.

THE GREAT CONTINENT of Asia teemed with dinosaurs during the Jurassic period. Asia was not as large then as it is today. High sea levels flooded some regions. The Indian subcontinent was still separated from Asia by thousands of miles. It would take millions of years to drift north, creating the Himalayas as the two landmasses collided. Europe and Asia were separated by a narrow strait.

DEFENSE AND ATTACK

In the middle of the Jurassic period, giant sauropods thrived in East Asia. One of the largest, Mamenchisaurus, was over 80 feet (24 m) long (and more than half of that was its neck!). Another sauropod, Shunosaurus, had a spiked club at the end of its tail for defense against predators. Tuojiangosaurus, a type of stegosaur, was protected by the spikes on its back. It used those on its tail to fend off fierce enemies like Yangchuanosaurus. Meanwhile, tiny Xiaosaurus took cover under low bushes, looking for ferns and other plants to eat. At the end of the Jurassic period, sauropods died out everywhere. Only in South America did a few kinds, the titanosaurs, live into the Cretaceous.

Yangchuanosaurus

Yangchuanosaurus was a deadly, 30-foot- (15 m) long meat-eater. Hunting in packs, it sought out the youngest and weakest in a herd of Mamenchisaurus to attack.

Tuojiangosaurus's plates made it look big and dangerous, but its chief weapon was its tail, which had four cone-shaped spikes at the tip. One swing of this tail could have inflicted real damage.

Mamenchisaurus

Shunosaurus

Tuojiangosaurus

Xiaosaurus

Yangchuano-saurus

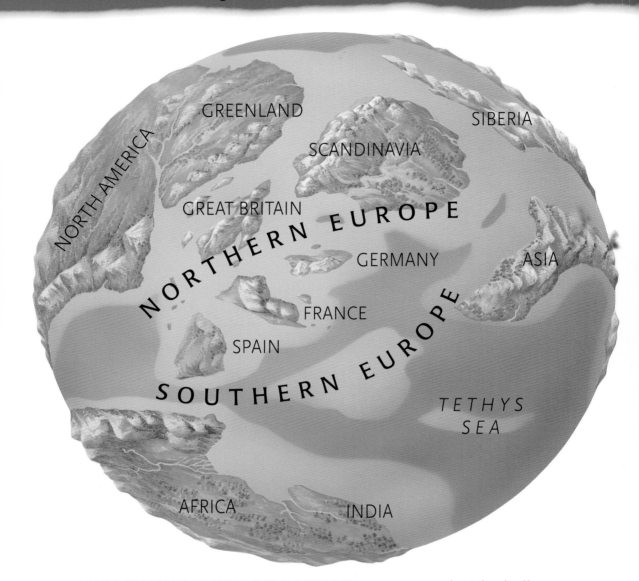

EUROPE IN THE JURASSIC PERIOD was covered with shallow seas, salt-water lagoons, freshwater lakes, and marshes. The continent we know today was then broken up into islands. The conditions suited only certain kinds of dinosaurs. Once dead, their bones and other hard parts became covered with sand, mud, or silt below the warm, shallow waters and eventually became fossilized.

BODY ARMOR

Scelidosaurus was was an armored, plant-eating dinosaur that lived about 200 million years ago in England, North America, and East Asia. About the same size as a crocodile today, its armor was made of bony, spiked lumps, called scutes, on its back, sides, and tail.

Archaeopteryx

Scelidosaurus

EARLY BIRD

Archaeopteryx ("first bird") is one of the earliest known birds. It lived in Jurassic Europe about 150 million years ago. Archaeopteryx fossils found in southern Germany show prints made by its delicate feathers. It also had a tooth-filled beak and a long, bony tail. Archaeopteryx was probably descended from small, feathered theropods called raptors.

Megalosaurus terrorized stegosaurs and sauropods in Jurassic Europe. A fierce 30-foot (15 m) carnivore, it hunted prey much bigger than itself, like Cetiosaurus, and snacked on tiny Echinodon.

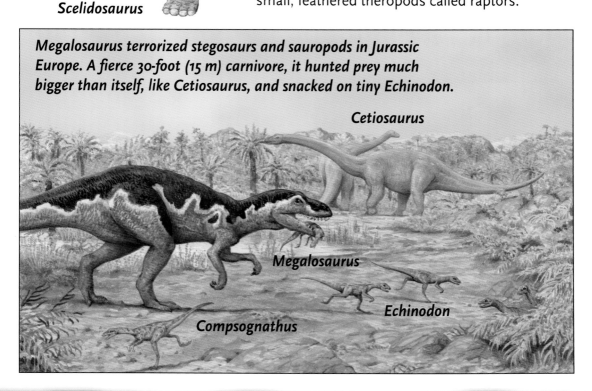

Cetiosaurus

Megalosaurus

Echinodon

Compsognathus

I N THE CRETACEOUS PERIOD, 144 to 65 million years ago, Laurasia and Gondwana finally broke apart. Shallow seas covered Europe and North America. Chalk rocks formed on the beds of these seas ("Cretaceous" comes from *creta*, or "chalk" in Latin). The world's climate became cooler and drier.

NORTH AMERICA

ATLANTIC OCEAN

SOUTH AMERICA

LETHAL ATTACK

Sauropelta was an ankylosaur, a plant-eater that first appeared in Cretaceous North America. Its tough, leathery skin was covered with bony studs. It also had long, sharp spikes around its neck and along the sides of its body. How could the small, child-sized predator Deinonychus penetrate these defenses? A pack would surround Sauropelta before rushing at it, leaping onto its back, and slashing its hide with the sharp scythe-shaped claws on the second toe of their feet.

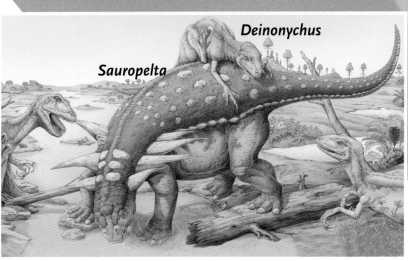

Deinonychus

Sauropelta

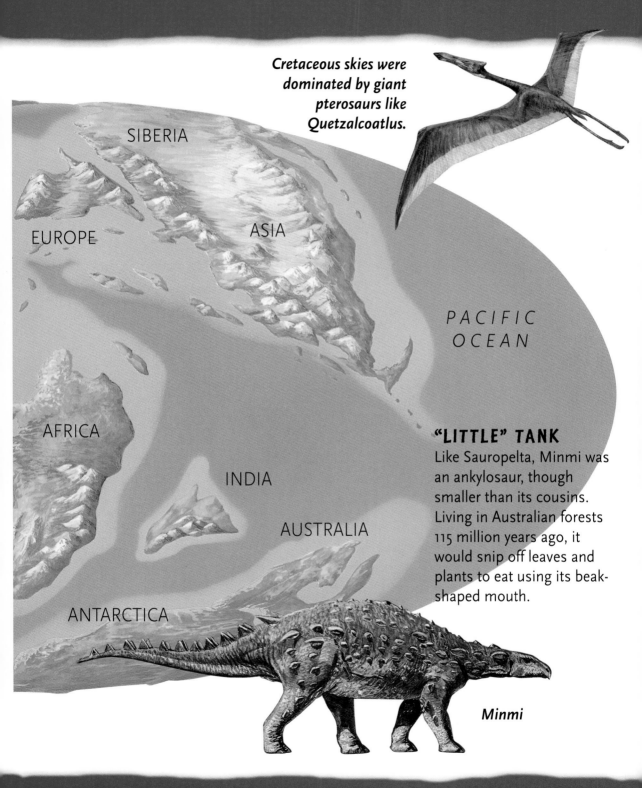

Cretaceous skies were dominated by giant pterosaurs like Quetzalcoatlus.

SIBERIA

EUROPE

ASIA

PACIFIC OCEAN

AFRICA

INDIA

AUSTRALIA

ANTARCTICA

"LITTLE" TANK
Like Sauropelta, Minmi was an ankylosaur, though smaller than its cousins. Living in Australian forests 115 million years ago, it would snip off leaves and plants to eat using its beak-shaped mouth.

Minmi

B Y THE CRETACEOUS PERIOD, North America had drifted away from Europe and South America, but it was still connected to Asia. Warm, shallow seas divided the continent into several large islands. The Western Interior Seaway divided it in half. The climate was warmer than it is today. On land, flowering plants and broadleaf trees replaced some of the coniferous forests on the continent.

CLASH OF THE TITANS

Triceratops was the best-known of a new group of plant-eating dinosaurs, the ceratopsians, that appeared in the later years of the Cretaceous period. Triceratops used its sharp beak to bite off tough vegetation. The long, pointed horns on its brow and snout, together with a huge, bony neck frill, gave it some protection against the monstrous 40-foot- (12 m) long predator, Tyrannosaurus rex, that lived at the same time. T. rex had massive jaws lined with saw-edged teeth, some more than 6 inches (15 cm) long. With its powerful legs, it could run fast over short distances. It would rush at its victims and bring them down with its teeth or claws. Its tiny arms could have been used to pin down prey.

Silvisaurus

Silvisaurus's skull had wide nasal passages. These may have let it make a booming call to others in the herd.

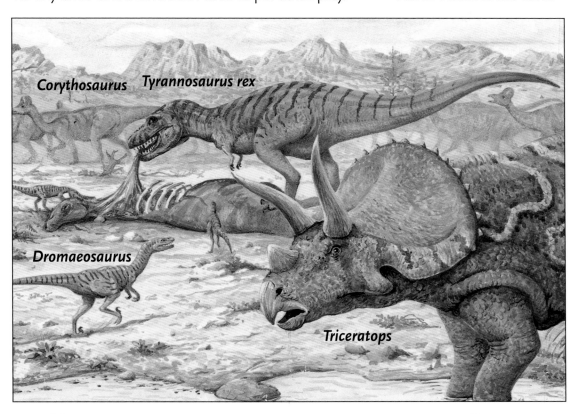

Corythosaurus Tyrannosaurus rex

Dromaeosaurus

Triceratops

Cretaceous Asia

A CROSS THE WORLD during the Cretaceous period, the oceans covered a much greater portion of the Earth's surface than they do today. Asia was the largest continent, and many dinosaur fossils from this period have been found in Mongolia and China, including those of feathered species. Southern Asia, where the Himalayas rise today, was a chain of islands in Cretaceous times.

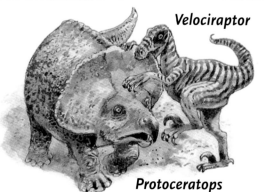

Velociraptor

Protoceratops

CRETACEOUS CRIME SCENE

An amazing fossil find shows two dinosaurs battling to the death 80 million years ago. Protoceratops, a pig-sized cousin of Triceratops, was attacked by the fierce hunter, Velociraptor. Protoceratops bit the attacker with its beak, while Velociraptor slashed back with its foot claws.

LIFE IN THE DESERT

Saichania was an ankylosaur. It was covered with body "armor" and a clubbed tail for defense. Its sharp beak was good for cutting and chewing tough desert plants. Another desert dweller, Gallimimus, was quite similar in size and build to a modern ostrich, but with scales instead of feathers. It was the fastest runner of its time.

Unlike birds today, Sinornis, a small Cretaceous bird, had teeth and wing-claws.

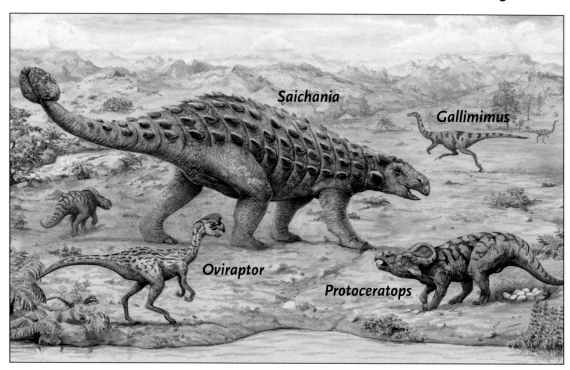

Saichania

Gallimimus

Oviraptor

Protoceratops

GREENLAND

NORTH AMERICA

SCANDINAVIA

RUSSIA

Future Urals

SCOTLAND

ENGLAND

GERMANY

E U R O P E

FRANCE

WEST ASIA

ATLANTIC
OCEAN

SPAIN

INDIAN
OCEAN

N O R T H   A F R I C A

TODAY, EUROPE has two main islands, Britain and Ireland. But back in Cretaceous times, Europe was made up almost entirely of islands surrounded by wide, shallow seas. Only the hills and mountains of Scandinavia in the north towered above the waters. Many new kinds of flowering plants and blossoming trees evolved on these low-lying islands, along with new kinds of dinosaurs to eat them.

SAFETY IN NUMBERS (AND SIZE)

The brachiosaurids were immensely large sauropods that survived into the Cretaceous period. Plant-eaters were always in danger of attacks from predators, but the brachiosaurids' huge size protected them from even their biggest enemies. Hypsilophodon relied on both its speed to sprint away from danger, and on safety in numbers by moving around in herds.

One of the largest pterosaurs that ever lived, Ornithocheirus had a wingspan of 40 feet (12 m). Its oddly shaped beak may have helped it cut through the water as it skimmed the surface for fish.

Baryonyx scoured the rivers of Europe looking for fish to eat.

PREDATORS BEWARE!

Iguanodon was a slow-moving, peaceful plant-eater that lived in herds for protection, just like Hypsilophodon, even though it was a bigger dinosaur. But if it was cornered by a hungry Acrocanthosaurus, Iguanodon stood up on its hind legs and jabbed its sharp thumb-claw into its attacker's neck or body.

Most sauropods died out in the Jurassic period, but some brachiosaurids survived.

Unlike many earlier dinosaurs, Iguanodon and Hypsilophodon could chew their food before digesting it.

Brachiosaurids

Acrocanthosaurus

Iguanodon

Iguanodon

Hypsilophodon

Extinction

DINOSAURS RULED the Earth for more than 160 million years. During this time, hundreds of different kinds of dinosaur lived and died. Some left their fossils behind in the rocks. Then, about 65 million years ago, they suddenly disappeared.

Marine reptiles, pterosaurs, many kinds of shellfish, and a huge number of other land animals and plants also died out. Three-quarters of life on Earth vanished forever. What could have caused this mass extinction? Scientists think that a large meteorite (above) hit the Earth. The resulting explosion created massive dust clouds that blocked out the sun's light and warmth.

After the meteorite struck, dinosaurs like Tyrannosaurus rex, could not adapt to the new environment.

The red bullseye pinpoints where an meteorite crashed to Earth at Chicxulub on the Yucatán peninsula, Mexico, 65 million years ago.

A very long winter began. Plants soon died, and with them the plant-eating dinosaurs that relied on them for food. With no prey to hunt, flesh-eaters soon followed. The Age of the Dinosaurs was over.

Or was it? Birds, the close relatives of small, feathered dinosaurs, survived, so it could be said that dinosaurs live on to this day. Another group, the mammals, also lived on. While dinosaurs ruled, they were tiny creatures scurrying about at night. With no predators, mammals evolved into the many different kinds we know today.

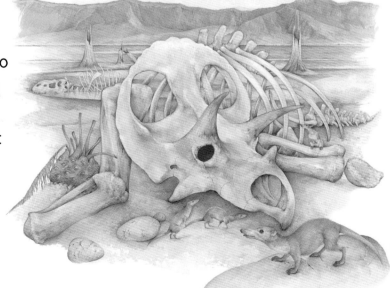

Discovering the Dinosaurs

ALL WE KNOW about the dinosaurs comes from studying their fossils. This science is called paleontology. Scientists can gain a lot of information from fossils, such as a dinosaur's size, the way it moved, and what it ate, especially when they compare it with how animals live today.

The place where fossils are found is called the "dig." Here, scientists uncover the bones very carefully.

Paleontologists work on a fossil of Tyrannosaurus rex. The best places to find such fossils are often deserts, sea cliffs, or quarries.

CAPTURED IN STONE

Fossils form when an animal dies and is quickly buried in sediment such as sand, silt, or mud (1). The soft parts, like skin, rot away, but minerals in the water fill up the spaces inside the hard parts, like bones, teeth, or shell, left behind (2). Over millions of years, layers of sediment build up, press together, and turn into hard rock (3). If the rock layer comes to the surface, because of erosion (4), the fossil may be discovered.

Soil is removed from around the bones with pick-axes and shovels. Pieces of rock are chipped away using tiny hammers, chisels, and scrapers. Loose sand and dust are carefully brushed away with toothbrushes.

At every stage, the rocks and fossils are measured, photographed, drawn, described in notes, and then taken away in plaster casts. Tiny details noted here can become important later.

THE DISCOVERY OF SUE

Finding a fossil of a whole dinosaur, with all the bones in place, is very rare. Sue was a fossil Tyrannosaurus rex found in 1990 with nearly all her parts present. Her skull, slightly crushed, is 5 feet (1.5 m) long. Being solid rock, it weighs more than 600 pounds (272 kg). Usually when bones, teeth, or other parts are missing, they can be "borrowed" from other similar fossils.

Glossary and Index

dinosaurs (DY-nuh-sawrz) Reptiles that lived on land 230-65 million years ago and walked upright on legs held beneath their bodies.

fossil (FO-sul) The remains of an animal or plant preserved in rock. A living thing becomes fossilized when buried by sediments and the spaces within its tissues are filled by minerals which set hard over time.

ornithischians (awr-nuh-THIS-kee-unz) The "bird-hipped" dinosaurs. Ornithischians had backward-slanting pubic bones, the lower part of the hip bone.

saurischians (saw-RIS-kee-unz) The "lizard-hipped" dinosaurs. Saurischians had forward-jutting pubic bones, the lower part of the hip bone.

sauropods (SOR-uh-podz) Long-necked, four-legged, plant-eating dinosaurs. They were the very largest and heaviest land animals of all time.

theropods (THIR-uh-podz) All the meat-eating saurischian dinosaurs.